STUPENDOUS SPORTS

RAMPAGING RUGBY

Robin Bennett

Robin is an author and entrepreneur who has written several books for children.

Aged 21, he was all set to become a cavalry officer (in charge of tanks), and aged 21 and a half, he found himself working as an assistant grave digger in south London wondering where it had all gone wrong.

Robin has played, watched and obsessed over rugby ever since losing both his front teeth in a ruck aged 12.

Matt Cherry

Matt grew up on the Kent coast, writing and drawing, where he still lives today with his wife and two children. He still loves to write and draw every day, so he hasn't changed much really. He's just a lot taller.

Conrad Smith

Conrad is a former New Zealand All Black who played predominantly at centre. He captained the Hurricanes and played for New Zealand from 2004 until 2015. He was a key member of New Zealand's 2011 and 2015 Rugby World Cup-winning teams. Following the 2015 World Cup he retired from international rugby.

STUPENDOUS SPORTS

RAMPAGING RUGBY

PRO TIPS BY ALL BLACK CONRAD SMITH

ROBIN BENNETT

ILLUSTRATED BY MATT CHERRY

Firefly

First published in 2021
by Firefly Press
25 Gabalfa Road, Llandaff North,
Cardiff, CF14 2JJ
www.fireflypress.co.uk

A CIP catalogue record of this book
is available from the British Library.

1 3 5 7 9 8 6 4 2

ISBN 978-1-913102-60-9

*This book has been published with the support
of the Books Council of Wales.*

Design by: Claire Brisley
Printed and bound by: CPI Group (UK) Ltd,
Croydon, Surrey CRO 4YY

FOREWORD

by Conrad Smith

*Former All Black and two-time
Rugby World Cup winner*

I grew up in New Zealand, where rugby is taught before you can walk. I had two older brothers, so our backyard was always a rugby field, and even the lounge when the weather was too cold. My dad played top club rugby, my uncle was an All Black, so every family gathering revolved around watching rugby, talking rugby and of course, for the children, playing rugby.

Rugby is a sport about which countless books could be written. And yet, as a kid who loved both rugby and books, I found very little to combine the two. Even now, as a father with a son who shares my passions, there seem to be very few books that shed light on the intricacies of this beautiful but sometimes complicated game.

Which explains why I'm excited to present this book to young rugby lovers throughout the world. A book to educate young players but also to entertain. To learn the skills to become a great player but also the values that make this a great game. This is a game that can be played by all and similarly this is a book to be enjoyed by all.

I have a lifetime of memories and a long list of friends thanks to rugby, and I hope this book will allow readers to both understand the game and appreciate all the opportunities rugby has to offer.

CONTENTS

CHAPTER 1: HISTORY

Who on Earth invented rugby?

Including why rugby balls look like rubbish footballs and how they killed Mrs Lindon.

Like most sports that involve:

 two **teams** that **hate** each other

🏉 a (sort of) **round object**

🏉 lots of **pushing** and **shoving**

rugby almost certainly started a very long time ago indeed – most likely when one group of barbarians chopped the head off someone (let's call him Bol) who lived in the village next door. Being barbarians (and it's no surprise to anyone that there is actually a team called the **Barbarians** today), they then started throwing poor Bol's head around for their own amusement, at which point everyone in

Bol's village ran around to put an immediate stop to all that fun at their expense. This may well have been the origin of the phrase '**can we have our Bol back?**'

The fight that followed usually went on for days, the head being '**passed**' **backwards** to make sure the other '**team**' couldn't get their grubby paws on it.

Eventually, both sides ended up in the village pond at which point they all realised:

- what a great time they'd had **knocking** each other's **teeth** out
- that chilling in a warm muddy **pond** with your mates is **ace**
- that no one had especially **liked** Bol in the first place.

Letting off a bit of steam in this highly entertaining, before-the-internet way was repeated in literally thousands of villages all over the place until chopping your neighbour's head off became unfashionable and everyone started playing football anyway.

Scroll forward a few centuries and we find ourselves at **Rugby School**, on the outskirts of the town of Rugby, in England. At a game of *football*.

It is the year **1823**.

Nothing about that day or the game must have seemed unusual, unless your name happened to be **William Webb Ellis**. Master Webb Ellis was a pupil at the school and no one knows much about him except that he decided to pick up the ball up and run with it.

Basically, he **cheated**.

ELLLISS!!!

However, instead of being punished by being hung by his **underpants** from the nearest crossbar, everyone on the pitch thought *now why didn't I think of that?* and pretty soon they were all at it.

> **NOTE** *There are some people who do not believe this happened at all, but everyone agrees that this version of rugby (ie one that doesn't involve a severed head) was first played at Rugby School and then introduced by ex-pupils to the rest of the world, where it caught on pretty quickly.*

By 1845 rugby had its own set of rules and ... *[drum roll]* ... **funny balls** *[cymbal clash]*!

FASCINATING FACT There's a rumour going around that **basketball** was invented to keep rugby players fit **off season**.

'Rugby is not a contact sport, it's a collision sport'

– Anonymous

Rebel girls

Women's rugby started a long time ago too.

The earliest known player is **Emily Valentine**.

In **1887**, at the tender age of **10**, she was watching her brothers play rugby and the call came for an **extra player**. Even though the idea of a girl playing rugby was about as strange as an octopus singing light opera, she got stuck in.

In **1991** the first **Women's Rugby World Cup** was organised by four determined English women, **Deborah Griffin**, **Sue Dorrington**, **Alice Cooper** and **Mary Forsyth**, and held in and around **Cardiff**, South Wales. Despite having little money and even less official support, 12 teams turned up

from as far afield as the **USSR**, **Canada**, **Japan** and **New Zealand**. The **USA** beat **England** in the final.

In a lot of **Asian** and **South American** countries the numbers of girls and boys playing rugby are pretty evenly split – **50/50**.

So, we're going to need more bullet points...

- **Forty per cent** of rugby's 800 million-strong fanbase is **female**.
- More girls have **started playing** rugby than boys in the past two years.
- The number of registered female players has risen to **2.7 million**, up from just **45,000** in 1995.
- Double Grand Slam winners **England** became the first fully **professional** women's team in January **2019**.

'We firmly believe that the development of **women in rugby** is the single **greatest opportunity** for our sport to grow in the next decade,' said World Rugby chairman **Sir Bill Beaumont**.

FASCINATING FACT Barette was a popular full-contact sport adapted from rugby union in the 1920s and played by women.

The ball

I think we can all agree that one of the most exciting aspects of rugby today is the fact that a rugby ball, passed by someone who knows what they are doing, resembles a **dangerous missile**. However, when the ball bounces, it behaves in a way that succeeds in making professional sportspeople look like **complete clowns**.

So, it can fly as smoothly as a rocket or jump around like someone with a small army of **bullet ants** down their shorts. This means that rugby is never predictable. Anything can happen and anything often does. This is **great**.

FASCINATING FACT During World War II, the Germans banned rugby as it was a bit too British and reminded them the British hadn't surrendered yet.

However, nobody thought about this 200 years ago – they just knew they wanted balls that were a bit **different** from footballs (mainly bigger) – and so they went to a couple of local shoemakers called **Richard Lindon** and **Bernardo Solano** and asked them to have a go at making one, since they were obviously good at stitching things together.

Nowadays, we have lots of things that inflate (mainly made of rubber, plastic or bubblegum). In those days, all they had that could be blown up and stay blown up for 90 minutes or more were **bladders** (the thing that keeps your pee from sloshing around in your tummy is also very good at keeping air in).

Obviously they couldn't use **human** bladders, so

they used the next best thing: **pigs' bladders**.

But bladders aren't round – ask any doctor (or shoemaker) – which meant they came out shaped like a **cucumber who has spent a lot of time in the gym**.

Also, some of the pigs' bladders weren't exactly fresh, and **Mr Lindon's wife**, whose job it was to blow the balls up, contracted a nasty disease from rotten bladders which unfortunately **killed** her.

At this point, Richard Lindon sensibly decided to start using **rubber** instead.

Great dates

🏉 **1883** The first **Six Nations** was played between **England, Ireland, Scotland** and **Wales** (so it was **Four Nations** before **France** and **Italy** asked to join in). At the time of writing, **Wales** have won the tournament the most times, while England have won the most **Grand Slams** (when one team beats all the others).

🏉 **1895** Rugby split into **rugby league** (paid players) and **rugby union** (not paid).

🏉 **1906 France** joined in.

🏉 **1907** ... then **Australia** and **New Zealand**.

🏉 **1954** First **Rugby League World Cup** (won

by **Great Britain**, beating France who, in embarrassment, or as a punishment, banned rugby league from calling itself 'rugby'. For years it had to called itself **Le Jeu à Treize** (Game of Thirteen), which was never going to catch on.

🏉 **1982** First **women's international game** was played between France and the Netherlands.

🏉 **1987** First **Rugby Union World Cup**.

CHAPTER 2: MEET THE PLAYERS

Why forwards play the ball back and backs go forward

Rugby loves you if you're **big**, it loves you if you're **small**, if you're **round**, **square**, or **skinny as a whip**. Whatever you are like physically, there's a place for you on the pitch and a job you can do to be **part of the team**.

In fact, the only thing you need to be able to play rugby is to **like it**. Being curious is OK, too.

There are **15** players on each side and they split roughly into:

- 🏉 **forwards** – the heavy tanks: **juggernauts** whose job it is to **crash** into each other and generally behave like hooligans
- 🏉 **backs** – whose job it is to make sense of all this mayhem with great **cunning**, fast **running** while – with any luck – avoiding bumping into scary forwards on their way to the try line – and glory.

OK, so who does what?
Glad you asked.

FORWARDS

These players make up the **scrum** or the '**pack**' and there are eight of them – so just over half the team.

NUMBER 1 LOOSEHEAD PROP **AND** NUMBER 3 TIGHTHEAD PROP

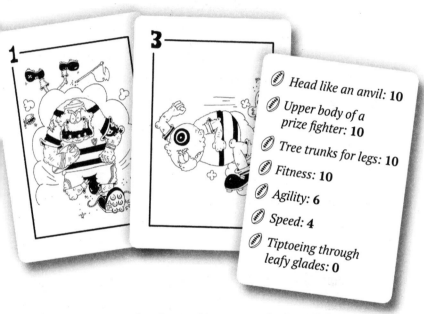

Head like an anvil: **10**

Upper body of a prize fighter: **10**

Tree trunks for legs: **10**

Fitness: **10**

Agility: **6**

Speed: **4**

Tiptoeing through leafy glades: **0**

The **props** are the **front line**, so it helps if they're good at looking terrifying. They need to be big but don't have to be tall. Basically, they are the team battering rams, so a strong neck is handy. You'll see them taking **short passes** and **charging** into the **opposition**, looking for weakness, tiring out the **defence** and **making space** for the **runner**.

Their jobs are to:

- 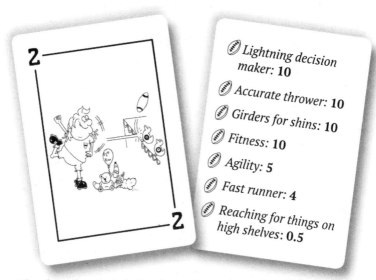 stop the **scrum** moving **backwards**
- support the **hooker** so he or she can '**hang**' between them in the scrum, the better to '**hook**' the ball out
- **lift** other players in the **lineout** and protect them so they don't lose the ball.
- They also need to **grab** and **hold** the ball for their side in open play after a **tackle**, which is why they also need to be surprisingly agile.

NUMBER 2 HOOKER

2

2

- Lightning decision maker: **10**
- Accurate thrower: **10**
- Girders for shins: **10**
- Fitness: **10**
- Agility: **5**
- Fast runner: **4**
- Reaching for things on high shelves: **0.5**

The **hooker**'s job in the **scrum** is to hook it out **faster** than the other hooker, so their timing must be perfect.

In the lineout, the **hooker** needs to be able to throw the ball to just the right **forward** at just the right time. So, although tough as old boots but perhaps a little on the short side, our hooker needs the **throwing skills** of a seven-foot basketball player in the NBA and the quick **decision making** of a fighter pilot.

When not **kicking** the other hooker in the shins in the scrum or lobbing balls into **lineouts**, the hooker is uttering blood-curdling screams while charging into the defence opposite. Another **battering ram**, part-time.

NUMBERS 4 AND 5 SECOND-ROW 'LOCKS'

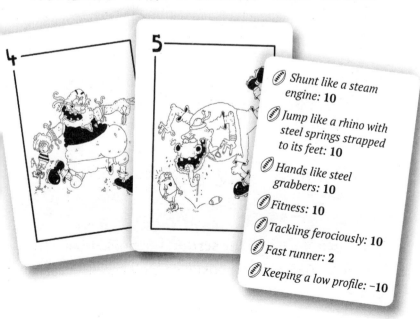

Shunt like a steam engine: **10**

Jump like a rhino with steel springs strapped to its feet: **10**

Hands like steel grabbers: **10**

Fitness: **10**

Tackling ferociously: **10**

Fast runner: **2**

Keeping a low profile: **-10**

Locks are the **giants**. When the camera pans across the players during the national anthem, they're the ones it needs to stop at and move up three feet to show their faces. Also, they always look like they're doing long division in their heads while they're singing.

They are the engine room of the scrum: the **high jumpers**, the fearsome **tacklers**, the lean-over-and-grab-the-(rugby)-ballers. If you can catch a wet rugby ball in one hand while someone is giving you an Olympic-standard wedgie, then you're a **lock**. Stand tall, be proud.

THE STRANGE TALE OF NORMAN BIGGS

Born in **1870**, **Biggs** held the record for being the youngest player to have an **international cap** for over one hundred years (he was **18 years and 49 days old**). He also holds the record for being the only rugby international to be killed by a **poison arrow** (serving in the British army in Nigeria).

NUMBER 6 BLINDSIDE FLANKER AND NUMBER 7 OPENSIDE FLANKER

All-round rugby Jedi: **10**
Quiet confidence: **10**
Turnover ability: **10**
Fitness: **10**
Star quality: **2**

Flankers are a bit like gums: no one quite knows what they are for but you'd sure as hell miss them if they suddenly vanished.

They used to be called **breakaways** or **wing forwards** because they **bind** with (hold onto) the **scrum** with just one arm and can break away with speed and ferocity to win loose ball or nail the **scrum-half** – or any one of a hundred other things they do in a match that no one really gives them much credit for or remembers afterwards.

Blindside flankers (touchline side, see **page 52**)

tend to be a bit bigger, with **opensides** (facing where the play is) typically smaller and quicker on the ball.

They are the **modest** giants, the players who are happy to stand at the edges of the group for the winning photo, not wave the cup about grinning like a chimp. It's fine, they're used to being on the **sidelines**, keeping it all together.

If you upset one, apologise immediately and hope for the best. However, if a **flanker** is your friend, count yourself very lucky.

NUMBER 8 (JUST CALLED NUMBER 8)

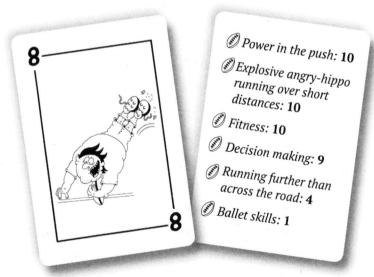

The **number 8** is far too busy to be thinking up fancy names for him or herself. They are like the

flankers' older brother or sister, and the only **forward** who is allowed to pick the ball up at the base of a scrum. This can be very effective if the **try line** is close by.

Seeing a **number 8** pick the ball up as it comes out of the scrum and push through to **score** will bring tears of joy and nostalgia to the eyes of any number of chubby old warriors with sticky-out ears who are watching in the crowd.

'Forwards win games, backs decide by how much'

– Anonymous

FASCINATING FACT

Japan's **Fumiaki Tanaka** is probably the **smallest** player to have played rugby at a top level. Standing only **166 cm tall** (**5 ft 4 in**) and weighing just **72 kg** (**11 st** and a bit), he is less than **half** the weight of the **heaviest** player to have played in a world cup – **Tonga's Ben Tameifuna**, who weighed in at a whopping **153 kg** (**24 st**) at the **Japan World Cup** in 2019. **Richard Metcalfe**, a former **Scottish** rugby union player, was the world's **tallest** ever international rugby player, at **213 cm** (**7 ft**).

BACKS

NUMBER 9 SCRUM-HALF

Hands of a magician: **10**
Quick thinking: **10**
Fitness: **10**
Star quality: **10**
Tackling backs: **5**
Tackling forwards: **2**

Being a **scrum-half** is a bit like living next to a squadron of **angry orcs** when you have a complicated job to do, where everything happens very fast and everyone is relying on you.

Nearly always the **smallest** and **lightest** person on the pitch, they also need to trust their **pack** to protect them from getting trampled into the mud by the other pack.

The **scrum-half** is the key decision maker when building an **attack**. They need to be quick with their hands, feet and brain. The **accuracy** and the **timing** of the pass out of the scrum is essential.

Mess it up and there's nowhere to hide, get it right and you'll be a hero.

This is why the **scrum-half** of a winning side is nearly always the one being carried about by cheering teammates and fans. That and the fact they're the only ones you can lift without getting a double hernia.

NUMBER 10 FLY-HALF

10

Ball-handling skills of a professional juggler: **10**

Fitness: **10**

Star quality: **10**

Tackling backs: **10**

Tackling forwards: **10**

Kicking: **10**

Running: **9**

Modesty: **0**

The **fly-half** is probably the most influential player in a side. Arranged on a pitch, a rugby team will often look like a snake: the head is the **scrum**, the **backs** are the flicking tail. The **fly-half** is therefore the heart of this attacking serpent.

Almost every play will go through him or her.

In an **attack**, they decide how to feed the ball to the **backs**, or whether to kick for **touch** or into gaps in the opposing team's **defence**.

In **defence**, they need to arrange the line of **backs** so that any attacking player has a covering **defender** who can make a **tackle** before the attack gets a chance to build up steam.

Fly-halves would probably make great generals: the type of general who is found in the thick of it waving a mace about and shouting rude words, not one who stands at the back with a telescope and a cup of tea.

NUMBER 11 LEFT WING AND NUMBER 14 RIGHT WING

Run like next door's cat being chased by a T-Rex: **10**

Fitness: **10**

Kicking: **8**

Tackling: **7**

Standing still … quietly: **-10**

Wing is a great position if you love everything about rugby except **tackling**.

Wings are known as **finishers**. Basically, you have to be able to run like your life depends upon it at a moment's notice.

And it often does.

However, for quite a lot of any match, a **wing** will be jumping up and down on the spot as if practising for an **Irish dancing** competition. This is partly impatience but also to keep warm while the forwards thrash it out in battle.

Loads of **tries** are scored by the **wings**, so there's that – the rest of the time you'll be shouting for the ball or trying to look busy.

FASCINATING **FACT** **Wales** invented singing the **national anthem** at the start of matches (in **1905**, they began singing in response to **New Zealand's haka**).

'I have enjoyed going to Twickenham more than I have enjoyed watching football'

– David Beckham

NUMBER 12 INSIDE CENTRE

Quick hands: **10**

Multitasking like a mum with a day job: **10**

Fitness: **10**

Tackling backs: **10**

Tackling forwards: **8**

Star quality: **8**

Kicking: **8**

Modesty: **5**

It's tempting to say the **inside centre** is a **fly-half** who wants to enjoy rugby without too much responsibility. However, by the time the ball gets to you, it's **mission critical**.

You are the start of the finish, the **critical link** between preparing an **attack** and carrying it out effectively.

The **scrum-half** has got the timing right and all the **forwards** are busy pulling themselves out of the mud, checking they've still got ears, the **fly-half** has given you a great ball and now it's up to you to use it.

There's still a lot of choice: either you can try and get through the **defensive line**, create a bit of space by **chip kicking** or pass to your (usually slightly faster) **outside centre**.

In defence, you have to be able to **tackle like a demon**.

NUMBER 13 OUTSIDE CENTRE

13

Run like mad: **10**
Ninja moves: **10**
Fitness: **10**
Tackling backs: **10**
Kicking: **8**
Tackling other forwards: **7**
Star quality: **7**
Modesty: **5**

The **outside centre** is all about running unlikely angles and timing. They have to have the same ability to **change direction** in the blink of an eye as a chicken in a hailstorm. **Outside centres** are probably very good at geometry.

By the time the **ball** gets to the **outside centre**, everyone is getting quite excited. We can all see what the **attack** options are, and the **try line** could be close. The **outside centre** does more or less the same job as the **inside centre**, except they can run almost as fast as a **wing** so, if there's space, they can gain a lot of ground or go all the way.

If you are playing **number 13** you will also know just the right moment to offload the ball to the **wing** for them to get over the line.

But you also need to know when to chip off the foot and be able to do so while running at full tilt without falling over, slicing the ball straight **into touch** or being charged down. Kicking into space so the **wing** can run on, scoop the ball up and score is one of the most satisfying sights in rugby. Unless you are defending.

NUMBER 15 FULL BACK

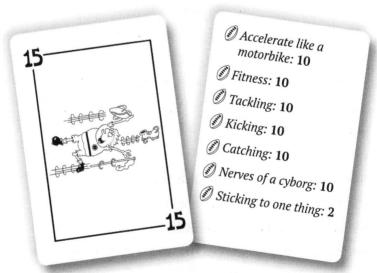

15

15

Accelerate like a motorbike: **10**

Fitness: **10**

Tackling: **10**

Kicking: **10**

Catching: **10**

Nerves of a cyborg: **10**

Sticking to one thing: **2**

What can I say? The buck stops with you. You're on your own. This is it. We're all counting on you.

And we're all watching.

Several times in most matches the **full back** will have to live that moment we all dread: someone kicks the ball **so high** in the air it fades into the mist and rain. As you squint up into the swirling, grey sky trying to figure out where it has gone and if it will ever come down, a noise like rolling thunder makes you risk a glance down the **pitch** ... and you very quickly wish you hadn't: barely 20 yards away and closing fast, a dozen very large, angry people are pounding in **your direction**.

They've no idea where the ball is either, but they don't give a monkey's butt – you're the **full back** and their target and they can see you just fine...

You swallow hard, look up and – to your everlasting relief – the ball finally comes tumbling out of the sky. You take several short steps, get underneath it and take the **catch**. The army of bodies is so close you can feel an approaching wind but you don't care, the world around stops: there's only you and the ball that matter. It's like the moment in *The Matrix* when Keanu Reeves figures out he can dodge bullets: you sidestep, wrong-footing an **attacking wing**, and then you're off, reaching top speed in just three steps. You may manage to get past a couple more players before deciding to **kick to touch** (especially if you're in your own **22** – see **page 37**) or you could **pass out** to one of the **wings**.

Or you can return the favour.

Kicking the ball as high and deep as you can, you see the **full back** on the other side go sickly grey with fear. Hee hee!

The **full back** is the last line of **defence**: runner, tackler, kicker and hero. On a good day.

SUBSTITUTES

Once upon a time, if you were on the **subs bench**, you only got a game if someone lost an arm or they got sucked into the bottomless pit of mud near the **halfway line**, never to be seen again.

However, these days being a **sub** is a big deal. In **international matches**, up to **eight substitutes** can be brought on, so you're very likely to get a game and often at a pivotal moment where you can dash on in a pair of clean shorts and run rings against an exhausted opposing team who have been on the **pitch** for an hour already.

Che Guevara, the revolutionary Argentinian, was a huge rugby fan and was a ferocious **fly-half** in spite of his asthma.

'Mothers keep photos of them on the mantelpiece to stop the kids going too near the fire'

– Sports commentator Jim Neilly, talking about the Munster pack

PRO TIPS

As an outside centre myself, I think this position needs a few more Top Trump 10s for the skill component as they are definitely the most important member of the team...

But the main message from all this is that rugby is indeed a sport for everyone ... and, while players are getting bigger, faster, stronger, I've still played with many tiny half-backs, stocky hookers, and wingers so skinny they would disappear in a strong wind. Growing up I was constantly told I was too small to play centre ... so I just made sure the other parts of my game were really good ... and then I made sure I had someone extra strong and powerful playing next to me ... Thanks, Ma'a [Nonu]!

Conrad

CHAPTER 3: THE MATCH

Why a game of rugby is 80 minutes long (except when it isn't), *the two different ways to score (except there aren't) and how to knock the living daylights out of the opposition (except don't).*

STRUCTURE

Actually no one knows why a game of rugby lasts **80 minutes**.

However, **test cricket** lasts five days because most of the time you stand about with your hands in your pockets, **golf** is usually all day and everyone gets to use a buggy because it's impossible to walk more than six feet in golf shoes without getting blood blisters. On the other hand, a **boxing match** is about 30 minutes, unless someone gets knocked out or runs away, and **karate** is over in less than 15 minutes – including all the bowing.

Therefore, the clue is probably in how **physical** a sport is.

Being a **contact sport**, **rugby** is considered to be a bit more tiring than **football** but a lot less tiring than, say, getting repeatedly punched in the face.

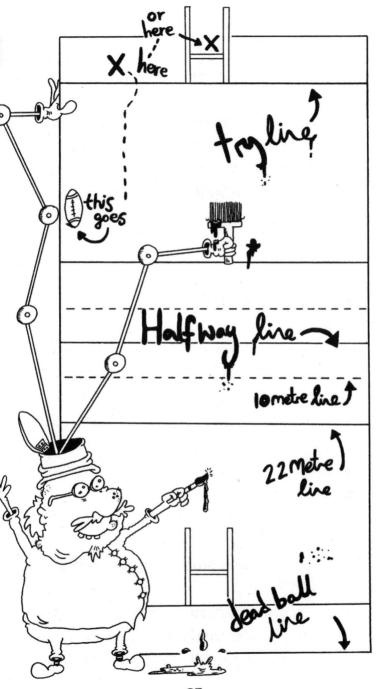

So **80 minutes** it is, then. This doesn't count **stoppage time** for injuries or a good ten minutes of a match when the **referee** shouts at the players.

Before a match starts, the two **team captains** will toss a coin to decide who **kicks off** (starts).

After **40 minutes**, the teams have a **10–15-minute break**, then switch sides to play the **second half**. The match is not over until the ball goes 'dead' (**into touch**) or the referee blows his whistle.

The winner is whoever has the most **points** at the end of the match.

Simple.

Switching sides at half-time is important. Rugby tends to be played in countries where the weather is **awful**, so having a blizzard or the baking sun in your face for 40 minutes is going to make life harder: getting to play in the other direction makes it fairer.

If the scores are **level** (drawn) at

dink

full time, then that is usually the end of it, except if there absolutely has to be a winner (in a **knockout competition** or **final**). If that is the case, then two **10-minute halves** are added and called '**extra time**'. If the game is still a draw after that, there can be a further '**sudden death**' 10 minutes added.

If there is still no winner, then there will be a

IMPORTANT NOTE *This is not actual death: it's just a dramatic way of saying the first team that scores wins.*

penalty-kick shootout to decide. Again, this is not an actual shootout. It's like in **football**, except England doesn't always lose to Germany in the semis.

SCORING

Basically, there are two ways to score points: by **touching** the ball down behind the other team's **try line** (this is the second-to-last line at the end of the pitch and is usually about **100 metres** from your own try line) or by **kicking** the ball between the **posts**.

However, like most things in life, **simple rules** always lead to more **complicated exceptions**, which is how a really easy game of cards like Snap! eventually evolved into Contract Bridge.

There are actually **several variations** on the way to **score** in a game of rugby, which is partly why it's such a fascinating game.

Try: 5 points

By running **forwards** with the ball (not forgetting to **pass backwards** and keep an eye out sideways), you eventually find yourself crossing the **try line** of your enemy.

ANOTHER IMPORTANT NOTE *If you happen to cross the very **last line** with the ball in your hand, you might as well keep going. You won't be popular with anyone on your team.*

*You'll know when you've reached the **try line** because roughly half the crowd (and your teammates) will be jumping up and down going mad with joy.*

*At this point you need to put the ball down firmly, while still holding on to it. This is **important**. If you forget to do this because you're busy grinning at your mum in the crowd or if you drop the ball, then **no points** will be awarded and you'll be sitting on your own in the bus on the way home.*

A **try** is the absolute best way to score (it carries the most points) and you'll be a hero.

FASCINATING FACT The **USA** have been **Olympic champions** since **1924** (91 years). This was the last time full-team rugby was an Olympic sport.

A FUNNY THING HAPPENED ...

George Napier, one of **New Zealand**'s greatest **full backs**, was refereeing a charity match when the ball popped up in front of him. Unable to resist, he picked it up and **scored a try.**

Conversion: 2 points

This is having the cherry on the cake ... plus your name in swirly icing. After a try, your **team kicker** gets a shot at kicking the ball between the posts. They must get the ball over the **crossbar** and between the posts. Also, he or she must take the kick in line with where you put the ball down for the try, so the **closer** you get to the posts when you **score** a try, the better.

Drop goal: 3 points

A **drop goal** is when you drop the ball on the ground and kick it on the **half-bounce** (or **half-volley**). Being able to score a drop goal is a bit like being able to rub your stomach and pat your head at the same time. You either can or you can't.

A **drop goal** is one of those hold-your-breath moments: everyone goes quiet and watches to see where the ball goes. As it tumbles though the air, as if in slow motion, the world stops what it is doing ... and waits...

Either it sails neatly between the posts and everyone thinks you're great, or it misses and the crowd goes back to eating their chips and complaining about the weather.

FASCINATING FACT The first ever **international** was between **Scotland** and **England**. Scotland won with a **conversion** and two **tries**.

'The touchline is the best defender'

– Billy Beaumont (In other words, when you're under attack and out of options, push the player with the ball into touch.)

Penalty kick: 3 points

If a **penalty** is awarded by the **referee** because someone on the other side has broken one of the rules, then your **team kicker** can have a shot at goal. In quite a lot of games, this is the most usual way of **scoring** and why you need a good kicker, and is also why you need to be careful about not giving away penalties. More matches are lost by **giving away** penalties than any other way.

Recently, **penalty kickers** have started going through some really very weird warm-ups before kicking the ball towards the posts. So if you see the kicker making chicken wings with their arms, wiggling their head like a camel that's fallen in love with a donkey, or practising ballet, don't worry: it's just their special ritual.

Penalty try: 5 points (plus 2 for the easy conversion)

If a team **deliberately** stops a try being scored by breaking a rule, then the referee can award a **penalty try.** To make matters worse (if you happen to be the team not playing by the rules), the other team's try is immediately awarded a **conversion** without have to kick the ball between the posts.

DOS AND DEFINITELY DON'TS

I've just made a list of 30 different things you can do **wrong** in rugby and I'm pretty sure I've missed loads. So I've given up.

Most of the time, it is the **referee's** job to spot **fouls** and **infringements**, and they need eyes in the back of their head – a bit like Yoda, or your mum in shorts with a whistle.

In big games, referees are helped by **touch judges** and even a **TMO** (television match official, or Person Who Prefers Not to Get Cold and Wet). In smaller matches they are helped by your dad hopping up and down, bellowing, 'Oi! Ref, forward pass, are you blind?' etc. from the touchline.

Instead of listing every offence – which would take ages – in a nutshell there are **four** types of thing you can do wrong:

- Something **dangerous** (high tackling, punching)
- Something that **stops play** (holding on to the ball after being tackled, collapsing a scrum)
- **Standing** where you **shouldn't be** (offside – being in front of the ball when your side is attacking)
- Being a **bad sport** (this includes arguing with the ref, or deliberately spoiling play).

This last one is important.

Rugby is a **tough sport**: it's a battle – but with rules and you're not allowed any weapons. It's practically the only sport you can play in anything from 30-degree heat where the pitch is like concrete, to driving rain in a sea of mud and torn-up grass, which is why it is played by over **8 million** people in over **100 countries**. Whether it snows, hails, gales or fogs, you're out there.

The ball won't bounce in a nice, sensible way and there's shouting and piles of bodies and you'll wonder at times if you can make it. Your ears will be ringing; bits of your body you've never even thought about will be sore, bruised and crying out for a warm bath.

But play it right – that means with **honour** and **respect** for your fellow players, for the **rules** and the **traditions** – and at the end of the match you'll have something that makes it all worthwhile: **pride** in **yourself** and your **team mates**.

A FUNNY THING HAPPENED ...

In **September 1949,** the **New Zealand All Blacks** managed to lose two **internationals** in one day when they sent two separate teams to two separate **tournaments** thousands of miles apart. One against **South Africa**, and one against **Australia**.

I started playing rugby when I was six, I retired when I was 36 and I'm now coaching ... I should know all the rules of rugby, but I don't. Nobody does. Not even the referees. But don't let that put you off. As with most things in life, the spirit is more important than the rules.

I was always told when I was young 'play hard but play fair' and that is rugby's number one rule. We run, we tackle, we try to break tackles but we never tackle high and we don't try to injure other players. We yell encouragement to our team mates but never talk back to referees.

This sportsmanship extends to the highest levels of rugby, and I look back with pride at the way players from both teams would meet in opposition changing rooms to shake hands and share stories soon after a tough test match. Equally, the fans who cheer loudly for their team sit alongside those supporting the opposition and for 80 minutes they are enemies, but soon after this allegiance is forgotten and the spirit of rugby prevails. As a player, following this spirit is most important, and you will pick up the more technical stuff along the way.

Conrad

CHAPTER 4: SET PIECES

The moves

WHAT'S A SET PIECE?

A **set piece** means all the players have to stop running around like their shorts are on fire and the ball's a bucket of water and form up into some kind of order. It is a great way to have a breather but the set piece is also a chance to show off what you've spent all week practising.

The set piece nearly always takes place after the **ball goes out** or for a **penalty**, or the ball has been **touched down** behind the defence's try line.

There are **two and a half** sorts of set piece:

1. The **lineout** (when the ball goes out of play)
2. The **scrum** (after the whistle has gone for a minor mistake)
2 AND A HALF. The **restart** (after a try).

THE LINEOUT

If the ball goes over the **sidelines** (into 'touch'), it means a lineout.

In the **lineout**, the forwards form up in lines

in order to try to catch a ball thrown from the **touchline**. This is a very useful skill for other things in life such as:

- 🏉 basketball during playtime
- 🏉 queuing in France.

So far so simple.

However, this is a sport made up by **schoolboys** with time on their hands, which means it's going to be a bit more complicated than that.

First up, where the lineout takes place is important and **which team** gets to throw the ball is **crucial**.

Who gets the **throw-in**?

- 🏉 The team that **didn't** make the **ball go out**
- 🏉 Or, whichever side's player was **not touching** the ball when it went **over the line**.

> **NOTE** If the ball goes out because a team has been awarded a penalty and kicks to touch, the team that has had the penalty awarded to them automatically gets the throw-in.

Where do the players **line up** for the lineout?

🏉 Where the ball **goes out**, stupid

🏉 ... except not always ... ha! Unlike in football, unless the ball **bounces** before it goes out, the lineout takes place where the kicker **kicked** the ball from, not where it **crosses** the touchline.

🏉 However, if the kicker is **inside** (behind) their own **22-metre line**, they can kick the ball straight into **touch** without the ball bouncing and the **lineout** is taken from where it crosses the touchline.

🏉 Also, if the ball is kicked to touch as a **penalty** then it does not need to **bounce**.

Other **lineout rules**:

🏉 The ball must be thrown **straight down the middle** of the two lines of players.

🏉 Players must not **jump** until the ball is thrown.

🏉 Players can go for the ball, but must not **grab** or **tackle** players on the other team.

🏉 Players may **lift** other players. This will normally be the job of the **tallest player** on the side – one of the **locks**. It might look like they are giving the liftee the world's worst **wedgie**, and they probably are, but there's not a lot else to grab hold of.

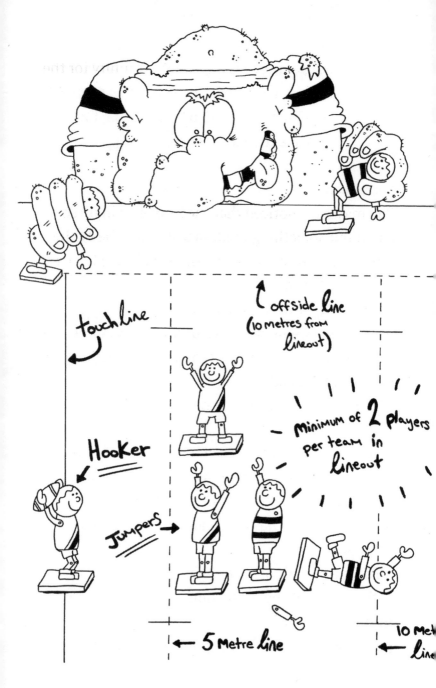

touchline

offside line
(10 metres from
lineout)

Minimum of 2 players
per team in lineout

Hooker

Jumpers

← 5 metre line

10 Met
lineou

Tactics

As I say, any **set piece** is a great opportunity for the teams to show off what they have been learning in training. As well as the '**lift**', here are some tactics they use to make the most of the **lineout**.

Secret codes

You may have noticed that the **hooker** will often shout out something random just before he or she lobs the ball into the eager (and very large) hands of the **forwards**.

It's nearly always something bizarre like '**Grannie's green bananas**' or '**Picklepuss999**' and it makes you wonder if the hooker hasn't had a bump on the head.

However, they haven't gone mad(der). It's a **secret code**!

This code is basically used to tell the rest of the forwards where the ball is going to go (officially known as **receiver selection**) and/or what to do when the ball has been caught (**post-catch selection**).

There are loads of different ways of coming up with codes, but the most common are **letter codes**, **numbers**, or the hooker might mention something **personal** about one of the players. Obviously they can't shout *Big Ears!*, *Smells like chips!* or *Bushy Beard!* It has to be a lot more sneaky than that. Or not ... it might be a double bluff ...

Once the ball is in the air, if the **attacking** side does everything right, the player who receives the ball can do one of two things: they can either **catch** the ball; **land** and **push forward** to form the spearhead of a '**maul**' (a loose type of scrum around a player on their feet, see **page 81**), bringing fear and mayhem to the other side; or they can **tap/pass** the ball back to the **scrum-half**, who will build a blistering attack of speed and great daring with his trusty backs.

So the **secret codes** are essential for everyone on the side to know what is going to happen.

Or, at least, what **should** happen – as you can count on the **defending** team having other ideas.

One of these can be the decision not to **compete** for the catch. Instead of lifting one of their giant **second row locks** up by the underpants, they get into a **defensive formation** in order to snuff out any **attack** before it can form.

While we're here, there are two other **attacking stratagems** you might like to know about.

The quick throw-in

This is when a player will **pass** the ball immediately after it goes out, in order to take the other side by **surprise**. It can be really effective but the rules are pretty strict:

- It can only be taken **before** the **lineout** is formed (ie before the players have started lining up).
- The ball has to go **backwards** down the **pitch**.
- The ball **cannot** be **touched** by any person (player or non-player) other than the person throwing in.
- It has to be **thrown** in exactly the **right place** (where or behind where the ball went out).

A(N) ~~FUNNY~~ AMAZING THING HAPPENED ...

In the **2019 World Cup**, the hosts, **Japan**, were not expected to go very far. A **Tier 2** side, they were up against two **Tier 1** sides: **Scotland** and, worst of all, **Ireland** – one of the tournament favourites to win. However, they beat both teams to go to the top of their table. The win against **Scotland** was particularly memorable as the match nearly didn't go ahead thanks to **Super Typhoon Hagibis**.

Throw beyond the lineout

Sometimes the **hooker** will signal that they intend to **throw** the ball **beyond** the **lineout**. This can be really exciting because one of the **backs** will then charge forward, dodge around the back of the lineout, receive the ball at speed as it is lobbed over the heads of the forwards ... and **race for the line**.

Or get **flattened**.

Because the problem with this is the ball takes a while to get to the **end** of the lineout, by which time everyone else can see where it is going and race after it – and the unfortunate **receiver**.

This tactic **rarely** works and often it looks like a mistake (like the **forwards** have forgotten to jump, for example). However, when the **attacking** team does pull it off, it's usually the start of something interesting.

So, the **lineout** can be a great opportunity to start an attack. But, like a lot in this great game, things can go wrong: the ball might not be **thrown straight**, it can be **knocked forward** by someone fumbling, the **ruck** (like a maul, see **page 81**) can **go to ground** and the ball might not be released, or there could be a **forward pass**.

Any of these **minor infringements** of the rules are dealt with by ... **torture!**

... only joking!

... a **scrum.**

THE SCRUM

Admittedly, there are quite a few of us who'd rather be **stretched on a rack** or threatened with **very hot forks** than find ourselves within a hundred miles of a **scrum**. Basically it's **eight** very large, **aggressively motivated** people pushing with all their might against eight other players who are just as big and cross. Then

someone perky (**scrum-half**) scurries around the side and lobs a ball in for good measure. Frankly, they might as well be lobbing a **cheeseburger** in, given the effect it has.

This – quite clearly – explains why a lot of kids in the olden days were **missing teeth** in their youth (author included) or had **ears** that **stuck out** from the side of their heads like a couple of stray satellite dishes.

In recent years the **rules** around scrums have changed and got a lot **stricter**.

Going into them in detail now would probably be **pointless** as they are very likely to change again before I finish this sentence...

But basically, they are all about making the game **flow** more **freely** and, above all, **safely**.

These days, **chewing** people's ears, **poking** them in the eye, **kicking** their shins and calling them **rude names** has given way to strict procedures about how the scrum **engages** (locks together), who can **push**, when they can push, how they can push, and keeping on your feet. Alright, there's still a bit of **imaginative name calling**, but that's half the fun.

If the teams aren't **locked together** perfectly or pushing against one another in a **safe way** (straight), or if it is in danger of **collapsing**, a scrum will be **stopped** immediately by the ref and a **penalty** may well be awarded against the side that did anything dangerous.

And that's **good**.

FASCINATING FACT In the **1999** match between **Scotland** and **Wales**, Scotland kicked off and scored in **nine seconds**, which is the **fastest try** in test history.

Uncontested v contested

Even now, some people are unhappy and think that all **scrums** should be **uncontested**. This means neither side **pushes** and the team who has had the **put-in** awarded to them automatically gets the ball and passes it out.

Lots of people think this is a good idea, because there is **no chance** of anything **bad** happening. Or **anything at all** happening, really.

Lots of other people (mainly people who **play rugby**) think this is bonkers and if you'd rather not let off some steam with a bunch of like-minded **sportspeople** who aren't afraid of a bit of pushing and shoving, then join the **ballroom dancing club**, where the worst thing that can happen to you is losing a sequin.

Anyway, what's the **point** of all this madness?
Well, I'm glad you asked.

Firstly, like the lineout, it's about **resetting the game** and gaining **possession** of the ball.

Secondly, it's about **territory**. A **dominant scrum** will be able to push the other side **over** the ball. A really dominant scrum can keep going until they **score**. This often happens when scrums are awarded on the **five-metre line**. Well, often enough to make it an outside chance and therefore pretty exciting when a **strong pack** goes for the push close to the opposition's **try line** – frequently in the closing stages of a match when they need a **try**, and not a penalty, to win.

This is one of the many moments in rugby when the whole crowd will be **on their feet**, or you'll be at home jumping up and down on the sofa shouting at the telly with bits of crisp flying out of your mouth.

'The difference between football and rugby ... in football the ball is a missile, in rugby, men are missiles.'
– Alfred E. Crawley

THE RESTART

Not traditionally a **set piece** but it has started to be seen as one. Once upon a time, after a **score**, the team that had just had five (or seven) points against them would **race up** to the **halfway line** for immediate revenge.

The **drop kick** would always be as high and deep as possible, and then the **reply** would nearly always be to kick it into **touch** for a **lineout**.
Players have got cunning now and have come up with a few ways of **controlling play** after the ball has left the kicker's muddy boot.

So there's:

The short kick

The ball has to go as near as possible just beyond the **10-metre line** and fairly high.

This is to give two waves of **chasers** time to rush the opposition. The first wave is usually spearheaded by one of the **locks** – tall, excellent catchers who will **contest** the ball (ie try and grab it off the player who is catching it on the other side).

The second wave (rest of the **pack**) will be there to contain the ball if it goes loose – usually because two opposing **locks** have not been able to catch the ball **cleanly**.

This is where the way the ball **bounces** is critical, and the fact that **anything** can happen just makes it all the more exciting.

The low kick

This puts pressure on the other side by kicking the ball **low** and **fast**. It's a good strategy to employ on a **windy day** and if the kicker can pick an **isolated** player, especially if they are looking in the wrong direction, tying up their laces or picking their nose.

The long kick

The most **common** restart kick, it is especially useful if you think the opposite team will **kick into touch**. If they do, it is very important to have a **lineout strategy** in place so that the ball can be **recycled** quickly and put into play to your **advantage**.

'He moves with the elegance of a cow on a bicycle'

– Frank Hyde on Noel Kelly

FASCINATING FACT

Approximately **40 per cent** of the power of a scrum is produced in the **front row**. In most professional teams, the **forward pack** weighs around **900 kg**. Other things that weigh 900 kg are:

- a small car
- 1,023 bunny rabbits
- A black rhino.

PRO TIPS

The set piece truly sets the backs apart from the forwards. In general play we all do the same things: we run, pass, tackle and even kick ... but when we get to lineouts and scrums, this is purely the domain of the forwards. And I am not exaggerating when I say that after all my life in rugby, after spending my whole career in the backs, I have no idea of what goes on when the whistle goes for the set piece.

I have a distinct memory of a test match I played in Cardiff where one of our forwards had been sent to the sin bin and the team asked me to join the scrum! I walked towards the scrum with my hands in the air explaining that the ball boy would be more use in the scrum, I didn't even know where to stand!

The scrum is a deep, dark place that no back is normally allowed to go near, while the lineouts and the intricate calling system are the most complicated parts of rugby that forwards jealously protect, well away from the curious eyes of backs.

But all of this takes time to practise and perfect, and it is a common sight across training fields around the world for the backs to be finished training, showered and leaving for home while the forwards are still practising their set pieces ... something for young players to keep in mind when choosing what position you want to play!!

Conrad

CHAPTER 5: BREAKDOWNS

How they happen, what happens ... and then what ...

This chapter is all about what goes on just before, during and after the **breakdown**.

Er, *breakdown?* Good question – and thanks for paying attention. A **breakdown** usually happens when a player is racing along without a care in the world, then someone else comes along and spoils it by **tackling** them. Two things happen immediately: the runner's happy thoughts of glory and popularity come to an abrupt halt ... and the **flow of the game** is stopped – ie there is a **breakdown** in **open play**.

What happens next is usually a **ruck** or a **maul**.

And this only ends when the **referee** blows the whistle for a **set piece** or a **penalty**, or when the ball is **passed out** and open play can continue.

> **NOTE** *The difference between a ruck and a maul: in a ruck the ball is generally on the ground, in a maul it is in the hands of a player who happens to be a) upright and b) conscious.*

1. BALL CARRYING

Unless you have an unusually **large mouth** (possibly because you're a dog), you've only got **two** basic options when it comes to ball carrying:

The **two-handed carry**. Or the **one-handed carry**.
  Each has its benefits.

Two-hand technique:

🏉 You're less likely to **drop** the ball.

🏉 It allows you to use the '**wand**' technique, ie '**figure of eight**' the ball about to sell a **dummy** (pretend pass) to the opposition.

🏉 It means you can quickly decide whether to pass **left** or **right**.

Two-handed carry

One-handed carry

Good grip on the ball

Keeps ball away from tackling players

One-armed bandit:

🏉 You can run **faster** with this technique. The ball is usually held in your **left hand**, tucked under the arm with your fingers making a sort of '**cage**'.

- You have a **free arm** to fend off **tacklers** or point over their shoulder and shout *spider!*
- You can **wave cheerily** at the **forwards** as you dash past.

Basically, it comes down to what you need to do at that moment. If **open play** means you are still in a **passing formation**, then **two-handed** is probably better. However, if you instantly need to run like your life depends on it (because there's a **number 8** breathing fiery breath down your neck), then **one arm** for holding the ball and one arm for pumping the air furiously is advised.

2. TACKLING

… is something you've got to get right for **everybody's** sake, not least yours. Do it **wrong** and it will **hurt**; do it **right** and it will feel **fantastic**.

However!

The object is not to **mangle** other players, it's all about **possession** and **territory**. So the main aim of the **tackle** is to stop the other team **gaining territory** in open play and (a big fat bonus) to **regain possession** of the ball.

It should also go without saying that you are only allowed to tackle someone who has actually **got** the ball. But I'm saying it anyway – just in case.

OK, **technique** first, then some detailed, but very necessary, **rules**.

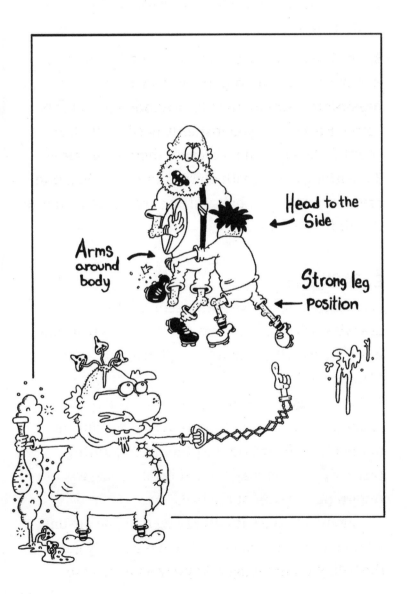

Tackle technique

Like almost anything you might be attempting in sport, at some point someone will shout at you, '**Bend your knees!**'

Tackling's a bit more complicated, because it's also extremely useful to be on your **toes** at the same time. Finally, keep your **weight forward** and your arms **stretched out** and wide.

Don't overdo it, or you'll just look **ridiculous** – like you're trying to run while carrying an

imaginary barrel of water.

Take it down a notch or two and you'll look like a **grizzly bear** that's prepared to run in several directions at once in order to hug someone to death.

So far so good...

The next bit is very important. If you're **tackling**, don't let the **runner** come to you (they won't, unless they're a massive **lock** and you're a scrappy **scrum-half**). You have to chase them down.

Eyes on your **opponent** (obviously), but don't look into their eyes, or at their arms or even their feet. Look at their **waist**. Firstly, because that is, more or less, where you plan to hit them. Secondly, the **hips** never lie. A runner will be flapping their hands, head and feet in all sorts of jinky directions to fool you, but the hips will always point in the direction they are going. It's **physically impossible** to do anything else.

Once you know where they are going, the next thing you do is **COMMIT** to the **tackle**.

You do this by **speeding up** for the last few yards. This is hard, especially if the player running at you is actually making the ground shake as they run: it's a bit like being told that the best way to deal with an angry hippo is to run towards it. However, it really is the **best way**. Trust me.

At this point, the runner will almost certainly **make their move** to avoid you – either by running to your right or your left. This is actually a good thing, as now you can tackle them **side on**, where there is no **weight** or **momentum** to knock you off balance or hurt you. You have to hit them **below** the chest, and remember: the lower you eventually get your **arms**, the easier they are to bring down.

Pick a **safe side** of their body to place your **head** – behind the **ball carrier**, if you can (so you don't bump them with your bonce) – and angle your **shoulder** into their **stomach**, sliding your arms down their **legs**, hugging them as hard as you can.

Crucially, keep your own legs **moving forward** all the time, pumping furiously.

Three things should happen if you've done it right:

- A **shoulder** in the **stomach** will knock the air out of them and weaken their **forward momentum** considerably.
- Your **arms** squeezing their **legs** will tangle them up and knock them **off balance**.
- Keeping your legs **moving forward** will take the runner to the **ground**.

As soon as they have been **tackled**, try to get on your feet as **quickly** as possible, especially if there is **loose ball** to pick up.

The rules of tackling

A tackle is only a **tackle** if the ball carrier is **stopped** and brought to the ground.

A **tackler** must:

- immediately release the ball carrier once both the players are on the ground (at least down on one knee)
- move away
- only pick the ball up if they are on both feet (and onside)
- let the tackled player release and move away from the ball.

The **ball carrier** must:

- immediately release the ball
- move away from the ball.

The tackle is only considered **over** when:

- a ruck is formed
- a player from either team gains possession of the ball and moves away or passes or kicks the ball (but remains on their feet)
- the ball is unplayable. This could be because the ball is stuck in a ruck.

FASCINATING FACT The **longest penalty** scored in a test match was exactly **64.2 m (70 yds)** against **Scotland**. It was scored by **Paul Thorburn** during the **1986 Five Nations Championship** at **Cardiff Arms Park**. The longest recorded successful **drop goal** is **77.7 m (85 yds)** by **Gerald Hamilton 'Gerry' Brand** for **South Africa** v **England** at **Twickenham**, on **2 January 1932**.

Break or avoid a tackle

In any other life situation – if you were minding your own business kicking a ball about in the park or standing at a bus stop – and a complete stranger **slammed into you** so hard that you fell over in a messy heap of legs and arms, you would be very upset.

But being **tackled** is going to happen in any rugby game and learning to take the knocks and get up with a **smile** on your face is a useful **life skill**.

However, if you can avoid getting tackled, it's good because you keep **possession** for **longer**, and the longer you have the ball, the more **opportunities** you have to **score**.

In fact, it's fair to say that **not being tackled** is kind of the whole **point** of rugby, so here are some tips for avoiding a tackle that don't **involve staying at home** or taking up **golf**:

Speed: run faster and/or change speed (slowing down or stopping).

Agility: change direction (no longer a sprint contest, it's alertness plus intelligence plus guesswork), so sidestep, jink, dodge etc.

Position: meaning position of your body – for example, if you lean into a tackle it makes you harder to stop

Hand-off (aka fend-off): Under 11, not allowed; 12–15, below the armpits only; after that, anywhere as long as it is stiff-arm (arm is fully extended before contact and is not a punch)

... and there's **kicking**.

'I don't believe in magic, I believe in hard work'

– Richie McCaw

3. KICKING OUT OF HAND

Is when you **kick** the ball while **running**. It's a bit **risky** because you **lose control** of the ball as soon as you've kicked it, so you need to think **tactics**:

Kick to touch

A good way of **gaining** a lot of ground quickly, but remember the other team get the **throw-in** at the **lineout**. Also, remember that if you kick from outside your 22, the ball has to **bounce** before it goes into touch (over the line).

Tactic: good option if there's no clear way of running the ball out of trouble.

Kick to space

Again, it gives you **ground** but you **don't** go for **touch** (to create a lineout). The aim when kicking long or short is to kick into the **empty space** behind the opposition's **defensive line**, which allows your faster players to run after the ball and maybe get to it first. It's exciting because **anything can happen** and great when it comes off.

Tactic: puts the other side in retreat.

NOTE *'Grubbers' – great name ... these are when the ball is kicked along the ground. A good grubber kicker can choose to kick the ball so it tumbles and can 'pop' up to be gathered by your quickest players or roll reasonably smoothly, so a player can touch down for a try.*

Kick high

Great option if you are one of those players who can make the ball **disappear** into the clouds and you've got one or two basketball players on your side. The **higher** it goes, the more **opportunity** you have for your tallest players or best jumpers to **steal** the ball from the other team, who suddenly find themselves having to stop thinking about tackling and start thinking about **catching**, in spite of the fact there's a horde of players running at them, **screaming**.

Tactic: *puts the other side under pressure.*

4. RUCKING (AND MAULING)

Someone who doesn't know much about rugby will look at a **ruck** and reach the conclusion that either a fight has broken out, or several very large **forwards** have decided to play *Twister* – and use the **fly-half** as the mat.

The **ruck** and the **maul** have real scope to go badly **wrong**, so here are some **dos** and definitely **don'ts**:

- When **tackled**, the ball carrier must **let go** of the ball, however tempting it is to hold on to it like your favourite **teddy** in a **zombie** apocalypse. **If you don't let go, it's a penalty**.
- Once **settled** on the ground, the ball carrier can place the ball **away** (behind) for his or her **teammates**. The tackled player should try to place the ball as **far away** from the **opposition** as possible and get their body **facing** their own team.
- Their teammates should **drive** and **clear** the **defensive** line of any of the opposing team if they can (the opposing team will almost

certainly be pushing the other way, so it's not going to be easy).

🏉 These **support players** must stay on their feet and push '**same shoulder, same foot**': keeping **low** and pushing like your ship is sinking and the only way to stop water coming in is to close a door. Once **defenders** have been cleared, all you little and big ruckers need to **defend** the ball by keeping low and making a sort of **roof** with your **shoulders**.

A **well-conducted** ruck will resemble a scrum that has been **won**, with controlled ball being fed out to the reassembled **backs** for another attack.

5. PASSING

Can be practised pretty much anywhere these days. You used to need a ball and another human being who was willing to pass it back (friend, enemy, parent, elderly butler...) Nowadays, you have specially shaped balls you can pass to yourself – all you need is a flat wall and deaf neighbours.

There are a few types of pass:

-  **Spin** (looks coolest, most popular type of pass these days, after it seemed to replace the flick in about 1973)
- **Offload** (mid-tackle)
- **Pop** (short and speedy)
- **Flick** (using wrists, hard to get wrong)
- **Reverse/blind** (passed back to front).

How to pass and catch

Pass left: all the power in the right hand, steady the ball with the left.

Pass right: (yep, you guessed it) all the power in the left hand, steady the ball with the right.

1. Swing your arms like a pendulum when you pass.

2. Look at the person you are

going to pass to (sounds obvious, but passing blind is one of the most common ways passes go wrong).

3. The receiver's hands should be up and in front, as a signal they are ready to catch the ball.

4. Aim towards the receiver's chest or their hands, if they are up.

5. If you are receiving the ball, it's a good idea to have a plan about what to do with it once you get it.

6. The passer and receiver should try to match their speeds.

A FUNNY THING HAPPENED...

In **2000** the **Dorchester Gladiators** – a small club from **England** made up of middle-aged men – went on a charity trip to **Romania** to give away toys to an orphanage.

When they got there, they were asked if they fancied a **friendly match**. Naturally, they agreed, thinking it would be against another small, local side and a nice way to finish up a visit to Bucharest. They began to suspect something was up when they arrived at the stadium to find **thousands** of singing fans and television cameras waiting for them. It turns out they had been confused with the **professional** invitation team, the **Barbarians,** and their opponents were the top Romanian club side, **Steaua Bucharest**, featuring many of their international players.

After a few minutes, everyone began to realise what the English players had known immediately. Typical of rugby, they saw the **funny side** and the match continued, with Steaua going easy on the elderly Gladiators. The match ended a respectable (and respectful) **60–17**.

'It is an incredible feeling to know that the Rugby World Cup is truly without borders'

 – Sergio Parisse. In his 142nd test appearance for Italy, he was watched live by Italian astronaut Luca Parmitano on board the International Space Station in 2019.

Unlike the set piece, the skills mentioned in this chapter are those that we backs love to spend time on. So, while the forwards push around the scrum machine and spend hours on their lineout, the backs take great joy in perfecting the spiral pass, landing a 40 m kick on a small handkerchief and competing against each other with sidesteps and evasion.

Practising and perfecting these skills is also something you can do at home, with family and friends in your own backyard. Unlike a game of rugby, which requires a large field and plenty of players, these skills usually only require a rugby ball or a couple of cones. And they are skills that often set the great players apart from the good players. The perfectly timed pass, the pinpoint kick, the textbook tackle: all the marks of the great players and always the result of hours of practice.

Of course, the best players possess what we call, a 'triple threat'. When they have the ball they can either carry, pass or kick, and they can do each action with great accuracy and the defence is never sure which option they will take!

Passing was something I always prided myself on, and the best advice I can give is to push your hands through the pass, so your fingers end up pointing at the target. This will always give you more power and accuracy with the pass, and it doesn't have to spiral!! Keep practising catching the ball and immediately passing in as little time as possible, a great skill to beat a fast-moving defence!

Conrad

'Rugby will always
hold a place of
pride for the
role it played ...
during those first
years of our new
democracy
(in South Africa)'

– Nelson Mandela

CHAPTER 6: RUGBY UNION IN THE FUTURE

800 million people can't be wrong

From Tahiti to Tonga, Scotland to Spain, Kazakhstan to Kurdistan, they're all at it. According to World Rugby, **rugby union** is now played in **120 countries** worldwide and it's growing in popularity in most of them.

Cool stats

It's time for rugby ball **BULLET POINTS**!

- In 1995 there were **1.5 million** registered players, now there are **9.6 million**.
- In the same year (1995), **50 million** people watched the World Cup ... fast forward 25 years, and in 2020, **878 million** fans were glued to their TV screens, dropping crisps on the carpet and throwing cushions at each other.
- **South Africa** has the most registered players with **651,146** and **England** the most players overall with **2,139,604** [*Wiki*].
- Rugby has a fanbase of **800 million** (that's the same number as all the people in Europe and the USA lumped together ... plus the population of Japan for good measure. Or 800 times everyone in Fiji.
- **Get Into Rugby** programme recorded over **2 million** kids starting rugby in **2018**.

[*Figures World Rugby 2017–2020*]

Safety

This is another aspect of the game that is **improving** every year, which

is a good idea for a number of reasons – like it being quite nice to leave the pitch at the end of a match with the right number of ears in roughly the right place on your head, but mainly because the **professional game** is getting **tougher** as the players get **bigger** ... and **better**!

The average player's weight has increased by almost **12 kilograms** (two st) since the first World Cup in **1987**.

This leads to the following equation:

A **20 PER CENT INCREASE** in player **HEIGHT**

= a **44 PER CENT INCREASE** in **STRENGTH**

= a **73 PER CENT INCREASE** in the size of the **OVERALL IMPACT**

= *OOOF!*

Height:	179.6cm	181.8cm	184.6cm	186.4cm	186.5cm
Weight:	84.4kg	88.3kg	90.1kg	103.6kg	104.4kg

But you need to be fast

... and they do not come much quicker than **Jonny May,** who recently revealed he set a new personal best of **10.49 metres per second** in a 40-metre speed test – faster than **Usain Bolt**'s average speed when he set his **100-metre world record**!

These days, **rucks** and **mauls** are stopped from going on for too long as they might cause **injury**. **Headguards** and **mouthguards** are worn and tackling is very carefully controlled to make sure it is safe.

Kids can only play **competitive**

rugby from the age of **six** and will play **tag rugby** (no scrums or tackling) until they are about eight or nine years old.

So, where next...

... *whatever the future holds*

Rugby is nearly **200 years old** at the time of writing this book, and yet whatever rules may change and wherever it is played and by whom, the **spirit** of rugby – the thing that gives it **heart** and makes it such a great game to play or watch – will never die, never change, **always endure**. It is **steadfast**, like its players. Rugby in all its forms will forever be the same fantastic fusion of **friendship** and **fair play**.

And **daring** to be **different**.

Just as when a ten-year-old girl threw off her hat and coat to **play rugby** with her brothers in an age when girls should only dance or sew ... or a boy called Webb Ellis picked up a ball, filled his lungs and **ran for the line**...

RUGBY IN THE YEAR 3000

Saturn Ringers Clash with Meteorites in Zero Gravity 7s

Hover Rugby Worlds Cup Won by Neptune Wanderers

Black Hole XV Swallow Up the Event Horizons in Unfriendly Friendl

Alpha Centauri Giants beat Pontypridd RFC

Which is hardly surprising, as they actually **are** giants

CONCLUSION

In my experience, rugby is one of the most **insane** sports you will come across, and yet it is played by some of the most **reasonable** and **civilised** people you could hope to meet. To an alien, it might look like a **fight** has broken out between **16** large, muddy people while **14** more slightly smaller people stand around watching keenly. It is **rough** and often takes place at a time of year when you would rather be indoors by the fire (**northern hemisphere** rugby) or indoors by an industrial air-conditioning unit (**southern hemisphere** rugby).

But even when I was at school, dragging on a sodden, filthy kit from the day before in a freezing locker room, I have almost **never regretted** a single game of rugby I have played – or watched, for that matter.

Rugby combines the best of team sport – being part of something to be **proud** of – with individual **achievement** and the **self-respect** and great sense of **satisfaction** that comes with that.

Plus, it's just **really good fun**.

COMPETITIONS ...
AND PAST WINNERS

'When you win, say nothing.
When you lose, say less'

– Anonymous

INTERNATIONAL COMPETITIONS

RUGBY WORLD CUP

When? Every four years.

Who's in it? The top 12 international teams (plus eight more teams from the regionals in the men's competition).

Since when? 1987 (men); 1991 (women).

Winners (and runners-up in brackets)

1987: New Zealand (France) *29–9*

1991: Australia (England) *12–6*

1995: South Africa (New Zealand) *15–12*

1999: Australia (France) *35–12*

2003: England (Australia) *20–17*

2007: South Africa (England) *15–6*

2011: New Zealand (France) *8–7*

2015: New Zealand (Australia) *34–17*

2019: South Africa (England) *32–12*

Teams with the most Rugby World Cup titles since 1987:

1. New Zealand – *3*

2. South Africa – *3*

3. Australia – *2*

4. England – *1*

SIX NATIONS

When? Every year.

Who's in it? England, Ireland, Wales, France, Italy and Scotland.

Since when? 1883 (men); 1996 (women).

SIX NATIONS ROLL OF HONOUR

Since 2000 (as the Six Nations)	**Since 1940** (as the Five Nations)

Since 2000
(as the Six Nations)

2000, 2001 England
2002 France
2003 England
2004 France
2005 Wales
2006, 2007 France
2008 Wales
2009 Ireland
2010 France
2011 England
2012, 2013 Wales
2014, 2015 Ireland
2016, 2017 England
2018 Ireland
2019 Wales
2020 England
2021 Wales

Since 1940
(as the Five Nations)

1940–46 Not held due to World War II
1947 England & Wales, shared after finishing with same number of points
1948 Ireland
1949 Ireland
1950 Wales
1951 Ireland
1952 Wales
1953 England
1954 England, France & Wales
1955 France & Wales
1956 Wales
1957 England
1958 England
1959 France
1960 England & France
1961 France
1962 France

1963 England

1964 Scotland & Wales

1965 Wales

1966 Wales

1967 France

1968 France

1969 Wales

1970 France & Wales

1971 Wales

1972 Not completed

1973 England, France, Ireland, Scotland & Wales

1974 Ireland

1975 Wales

1976 Wales

1977 France

1978 Wales

1979 Wales

1980 England

1981 France

1982 Ireland

1983 France & Ireland

1984 Scotland

1985 Ireland

1986 France & Scotland

1987 France

1988 France & Wales

1989 France

1990 Scotland

1991 England

1992 England

1993 France

1994 Wales

1995 England

1996 England

1997 France

1998 France

1999 Scotland

Wales and **England** hold **39** victories each (**27** outright and **12** shared for **Wales** to **England's 29** outright and **10** shared). Since the **Six Nations** era started in **2000**, only **Italy** and **Scotland** have failed to win the title.

THE RUGBY CHAMPIONSHIP
(FORMERLY TRI-NATIONS UNTIL ARGENTINA'S PUMAS STEPPED IN)

When? Every year.

Who's in it? Australia, New Zealand, South Africa and Argentina.

Since when? 1996.

WORLD RUGBY PACIFIC NATIONS CUP

When? Every year.

Who's in it? Fiji, Samoa, Tonga.

Since when? 2006.

MAJOR CLUB AND PROVINCIAL TOURNAMENTS

EUROPEAN RUGBY CHAMPIONS CUP

When? Every year.

Who's in it? Top clubs in Europe from those countries that compete in the Six Nations.

Since when? 1995 (when it was called the Heineken Cup).

INTERNATIONAL TROPHIES

The trophies in this list are regularly contested between two nations. Some of the competitions for these trophies form part of other international tournaments, such as the **Six Nations** and **The Rugby Championship**.

SIX NATIONS TROPHIES

- **Six Nations Championship Trophy**, since 1993
- **Triple Crown Trophy**, since 2006
- **Calcutta Cup** – England and Scotland, since 1879
- **Centenary Quaich** – Ireland and Scotland, since 1989
- **Millennium Trophy** – England and Ireland, since 1988
- **Giuseppe Garibaldi Trophy** – France and Italy, since 2007
- **Auld Alliance Trophy** – Scotland and France, since 2018

TROPHIES IN THE RUGBY CHAMPIONSHIP

- **Bledisloe Cup** – Australia and New Zealand, since 1931
- **Mandela Challenge Plate** – Australia and South Africa, since 2000
- **Freedom Cup** – New Zealand and South Africa,

since 2004

 Puma Trophy – Argentina and Australia, since 2000

OTHER TROPHIES

 Anexartisias Cup (Independence Cup) – Cyprus and Greece

 Antim Cup – Georgia and Romania

 Cook Cup – Australia and England

 Dave Gallaher Trophy – France and New Zealand

 Elgon Cup – Kenya and Uganda

 Hillary Shield – England and New Zealand

 Hopetoun Cup – Australia and Scotland

 James Bevan Trophy – Australia and Wales

 Lansdowne Cup – Australia and Ireland

 Prince William Cup – South Africa and Wales

 Trophée des Bicentenaires – Australia and France

 Tom Richards Trophy – Australia and the British and Irish Lions

 Raeburn Shield – hypothetical world title shield

MAJOR LEAGUES

International **rugby union** teams (decided on by **World Rugby**) ... and some of our favourite **nicknames.**

Note: All Tier 1 and Tier 2 sides must have played in a World Cup.

TIER 1 TEAMS

Argentina
('The Pumas')

Australia
('The Wallabies' and 'Wallaroos' for the women's team)

England ('The Red and Whites' and 'Red Roses' for the women's team)

France ('Les Bleus', or 'The Blues')

Ireland

Italy

New Zealand ('The All Blacks' and 'Black Ferns' for the women's team)

Scotland

South Africa ('The Springboks')

Wales

TIER 2 TEAMS

Canada ('The Canucks')

Fiji ('Bati' or 'The Warriors')

Georgia ('The Lelos' after a local sport that is very much like rugby)

Japan ('The Brave Blossoms')

Namibia

Portugal ('Os Lobos' or 'The Wolves')

Romania

Russia ('The Bears')

Samoa

Spain

Tonga

United States

Uruguay

TIER 3 (DEVELOPMENT ONE) TEAMS

Belgium

Brazil

Chile

Germany

Hong Kong ('The Dragons')

Ivory Coast

Kenya ('The Simbas')

South Korea

Zimbabwe ('The Sables')

TIER 3 (DEVELOPMENT TWO) TEAMS

- American Samoa
- Andorra
- Armenia
- Austria
- Azerbaijan
- Bahamas
- Barbados
- Bermuda
- Bosnia and Herzegovina
- Botswana
- British Virgin Islands
- Brunei
- Bulgaria
- Burundi
- Cambodia
- Cameroon
- Cayman Islands
- China
- Chinese Taipei
- Colombia
- Cook Islands
- Costa Rica
- Croatia
- Cyprus
- Czech Republic
- Denmark
- Eswatini
- Finland
- Ghana
- Greece
- Guam
- Guyana
- Hungary
- India
- Indonesia
- Iran
- Israel
- Jamaica
- Kazakhstan
- Kyrgyzstan
- Laos
- Latvia
- Lithuania
- Luxembourg
- Madagascar
- Malaysia
- Mali

Malta	Singapore
Mauritania	Slovenia
Mauritius	Solomon Islands
Mexico	Sri Lanka
Moldova	St Lucia
Monaco	St Vincent and the
Mongolia	Grenadines
Morocco	Sweden
Netherlands	Switzerland
Nigeria	Tahiti
Niue	Tanzania
Norway	Thailand
Pakistan	Togo
Panama	Trinidad and Tobago
Papua New Guinea	Tunisia
Paraguay	Uganda
Peru	Ukraine
Philippines	United Arab Emirates
Poland	Uzbekistan
Rwanda	Vanuatu
Senegal	Venezuela
Serbia	Zambia

FRENCH RUGBY FEDERATION

Mayotte

Réunion

Guadeloupe

Martinique

New Caledonia

Wallis and Futuna

NOT AFFILIATED TO WORLD RUGBY

Algeria

Benin

Basque Country

Burkina Faso

Catalonia

Central Africa

Chad

Congo

Curaçao

Democratic Republic of the Congo

Dominican Republic

Ecuador

El Salvador

Egypt

Estonia

Gabon

Galicia

Gibraltar

Guatemala

Jordan

Lebanon

Libya

Macau

Montenegro

Niger

Qatar

San Marino

Slovakia

St Kitts and Nevis

Turkey

Turks and Caicos Islands

Tuvalu

COMBINATION TEAMS

African Leopards : Pacific Islanders
British and Irish Lions : South American XV

DEFUNCT TEAMS

Arabian Gulf : East Germany
Commonwealth of : Nyasaland (Malawi)
Independent States : Soviet Union
Czechoslovakia : West Germany
East Africa : Yugoslavia

KEYWORDS
& WHAT THEY MEAN

22: The 22-metre line, marking 22 metres (72 ft) from the try line.

89: An '89' or eight-nine move is when the number 8 picks up the ball and short passes it to number 9 (scrum-half).

Advantage: 'Advantage' is a short period of time

after a team has broken a minor rule in which the other side has the opportunity to gain ground or tactical advantage, so the ref doesn't stop the game.

Ankle tap: An ankle tap or tap tackle is when you bring down a player going at full tilt by tapping their ankle – or tripping them up. It's extremely satisfying and very amusing to watch the expression on the face of the player who has been tap-tackled.

Bill: Australian name given to the Webb Ellis Cup (the Rugby World Cup trophy). Webb Ellis's first name was William – hence Bill.

Black dot: A black mark in the centre of the crossbar connecting the goal posts. It is there to help kickers with their aiming.

Blindside: The side of the pitch with the least space during a scrum or a breakdown in play.

Blitz defence: Borrowed from rugby league, the blitz defence is when the whole defensive line steam forward towards their marked man as one, as soon as the ball leaves a ruck or maul. It's meant to be scary and it usually is.

Blood bin: A player who is bleeding can be replaced for up to 15 minutes to mop up the blood, stitch the nose back on...

Box kick: This is typically when the scrum-half kicks the ball from behind the scrum back over into space behind the opposition that their team can pile into and gain territory.

Cavalry charge: No horses are actually involved. Often, during a penalty kick or free kick, the attacking players make a line behind their kicker. Upon a pre-arranged signal, they charge forward. The kicker then tap-kicks the ball and passes to one of the players behind.

Charge-down: When a kicker's ball is not cleared but caught or blocked by a player on the other side leaping like a salmon into the air (a salmon with arms, admittedly). It often results in a spectacular reversal of fortune, as in a try.

Choke tackle: Tackle in which the tackler tries to keep the ball carrier on their feet and push them backwards before grounding them. Tough to pull off but gives the tackler's side a gain in territory.

Cibi: A Fijian war dance performed by the Fiji national team before an international. Terrifying.

Crash ball: Grab a pass and charge the opposition's defensive line. The idea is to take out two or more defenders and create a yawning hole in the defence. Just don't try it if you're the scrum-half.

Drift defence: Forces the attacking side into a bottleneck near to the touchline. The defence moves forward and diagonally, following the path of the attacking side's passes. If used successfully, the ball will usually end up in the attacking winger's hands and, with nowhere to go, they can be pushed into touch.

Dummy pass: A cunning attacking plan used by generations of schoolchildren, where the ball carrier pretends to pass the ball to a teammate, but then continues to run with the ball. The aim is to trick defenders into covering the would-be pass receiver, creating a gap for the ball carrier to run into. If it is successful, the player is said to have 'sold a dummy'.

Dump tackle: The tackler wraps his arms around the ball carrier's thighs and runs along with him or her a short distance before 'dumping' them unceremoniously on the ground. The tackler must go to ground with the ball carrier for the tackle to be legal. It's more than a little embarrassing if you're the one being tackled but very amusing for everyone else.

Fend (or hand-off): Fending is the action by the ball carrier of repelling a tackler using his arm. For the action to be legal, the ball carrier's arm must be straight before contact is made and the hand open (not like a fist); a shove or 'straight-arm smash', where the arm is extended immediately before contact, is called a punch and obviously not allowed.

Full house: Scoring a try, conversion, penalty and drop goal in the same match. Basically your name has to be Jonny Wilkinson or Dan Carter.

Gain line: The gain line is the imaginary line (in the referee's head) drawn across the centre of the pitch when there is a breakdown in open play, such as a ruck, maul or scrum. Crossing the gain line represents a gain in territory.

Garryowen: Named after the Garryowen Football Club that first used this tactic, the garryowen, up-and-under kick or 'bomb' is when the kicker kicks the ball into the stratosphere to land, still glowing from re-entry, onto or behind the defending team.

Goose step: A goose step, originally used by Australian David Campese, is a running technique where the player slows down and takes a small 'hop' into the air before sprinting off – sometimes in a different direction. It looks absurd but is very effective.

Grubber kick: Makes the ball roll, skid and tumble across the ground, producing irregular bounces that make it more likely that whoever catches will knock on. If the ball 'sits up' it means it is in a perfect catching position.

Haka: A traditional Māori dance performed by New Zealand national teams prior to international matches. Better known than, but just as alarming as, the Fijian Cibi.

Hospital pass: Any pass that is made which has the inevitable, unavoidable consequence of the receiver being tackled, and usually very hard. Not nice.

Kick tennis: When both teams repeatedly kick from hand to the opposition, rather than running at the opposition and risking a turnover. Dull.

Latcher/Latching on: A latcher is a player who grabs hold of the ball carrier (on their team) like a baby limpet clinging to its mum on the first day of school, in order to add their power and weight and try to break the defence line or gain yards.

Mark: A mark is the place where the game will restart after a stoppage. *Note:* 'To call a mark' is different. It is 'called' by the player catching the ball if they are standing in their own 22, on both feet, when they receive a kick, and means they cannot be tackled. They must shout 'Mark!' extremely loudly for it to have any chance of working.

Maul: When a ball carrier is stopped (without being tackled) by an opposing player and a player from his own team latches on, it is officially a maul.

If the ball does not come out pronto, the referee will award a scrum to the team that did not take the ball into the maul.

Off load pass: A short pass made by a player being tackled just before he or she hits the ground.

On the full: If the ball is kicked into touch without first bouncing inside the field of play, it is on the full.

Overlap: When there are more attacking players on one side of the field than there are defenders. When a TV commentator says there's an overlap, your mum and dad will jump up and start waving their arms at the screen and shouting.

Phase: A phase is the time a ball is in play between breakdowns.

Pop pass: A very short pass. Not a pass from your grandpa.

Professional foul: A professional foul is a deliberate foul, usually to prevent an opponent scoring. It is punishable by a yellow card at least.

Red card: Red cards are shown by the referee to players who have been ordered off the pitch. The player will not be replaced. This takes place when a player is guilty of a serious foul or violent conduct, or for committing two offences resulting in cautions (yellow cards).

Red zone: This is a term used to describe the area of the pitch between the try line and around 22 metres out, in which it is most likely a try may be scored or conceded.

Shoeing: Players on their feet in a ruck sometimes encourage players on the ground to move away from the ball by kicking or raking them. This is illegal and will result in penalties and yellow or red cards.

Sin bin: Where a player must remain for a minimum of ten minutes after being shown a yellow card. Not actually a bin – just a bench.

Sipi Tau: Sipi Tau is a Tongan war dance performed

by the Tonga national team before each of their international matches.

Siva Tau: Siva Tau is a Samoan war dance performed by the Samoa national team before each of their international matches.

Spear tackle: A spear tackle is extremely dangerous. A player is picked up by the tackler and turned so that they are upside down. The tackler then drops or drives the player into the ground often head, neck or shoulder first, like driving a spear into the ground. Illegal and highly dangerous and can result in lengthy playing bans. Rightly so.

TMO: Television match official, commonly called the video referee.

Truck and trailer: Term for an accidental obstruction (getting in the way of an opponent who doesn't have the ball) in a maul. If the incident of truck and trailer is judged to be deliberate or the

latest in a series of similar infringements, a penalty may be awarded.

Turnover: When a team loses possession of the ball at the breakdown, then it's a turnover for the other team. Can be a sign of one team's pack dominating another. A team that regularly turns over the ball during a game will often go on to win.

Use it or lose it: If a maul stops moving forward the referee will often shout 'use it or lose it' to the team in possession of the ball. They've then got five seconds to pass the ball out of the maul. If they do not, then it's a scrum for the team not in possession at the beginning of the maul.

Wheeling: When a scrum turns through 90 degrees. It then is reset, with the ball being turned over (given to the other side to put in) if the ref decides the attacking team has deliberately or repeatedly wheeled the scrum.

OTHER TITLES IN THE STUPENDOUS SPORTS SERIES OUT SHORTLY:

FANTASTIC FOOTBALL

ROBIN BENNETT

ILLUSTRATED BY MATT CHERRY

Second in the comedy series **Savage Sports** which aims to do for **PE** what Horrible Histories did for **Year 7 History** with Mr Simkin.

⚽ Out in time for the **World Cup 2022**
⚽ Foreword and tips by a famous **football star**
⚽ 'Training Shorts' on YouTube and **www.stupendoussports.com**

DID YOU KNOW?

 That the earliest form of **football** started in **China** over **2200** years ago. It was called **Cuju** and involved **kicking** the ball into a net without using your **hands**.

In fact there is evidence that football was played in many parts of the world. In **1586** an **English explorer** called **John Davis** came across a tribe of **Inuits** (native people of **Greenland**) playing the game, stopped his ship and joined in.

Modern football **rules** were made up by **English schoolchildren** in the **19th century**.

Football wasn't always that **popular**. It was **banned** in a lot of countries – officially in **Scotland** until **1906**.

Football is easily the most popular sport in the **world**. According to **FIFA**, there are over **250 million players** playing in **200 countries** with over **3.5 billion fans** – nearly half the people in the world!

OTHER TITLES IN THE STUPENDOUS SPORTS SERIES OUT SHORTLY:

COOL CRICKET

ROBIN BENNETT

ILLUSTRATED BY
MATT CHERRY

Each chapter will have
cartoons, player tips
your coach won't tell you,
explanations, fascinating
facts and - yes - **funny
stories**. It will hopefully
teach you just
as much about
the **spirit** of the
game as the
rules.

◯ Out in time for the **ICC World Cup 2023**
◯ Foreword and tips by a **famous cricketer**
◯ **'Training Shorts'** on YouTube and
   www.stupendoussports.com

DID YOU KNOW?

- **Cricket** is thought to have started as a way for **English shepherds** to pass the time whilst looking after **sheep**, who were the first **fielders** and probably no worse at it than your little brother.

- Although it started in **16th Century** in **England**, a game in **Aleppo** in **Syria** was written about in **1676**! And the first ever **international** was played between the **US** and **Canada** in **New York in 1844**.

- **Test cricket** is one of the **longest** games in the world (normally **5 days**). The longest match ever was between **England** and **South Africa** – it went on for **2 weeks**!

- It is estimated that there are nearly **60 million players** of cricket in the world with over **2 billion fans,** which makes it the **second most popular** sport in the world after football. It is played in over **100 countries**. ▽

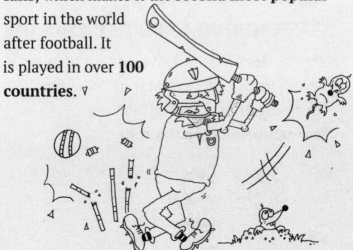

WWW.STUPENDOUSSPORTS.COM

THE PLACE FOR KIDS
WHO ARE MAD ON SPORT!

- SPORTS NEWS FOR KIDS
- BOOK AUTHOR VISITS
- CARTOONS
- FUNNY STORIES
- AUDIO DOWNLOADS AND VIDEOS
- NEWS ON FORTHCOMING EVENTS

STUPENDOUS SPORTS FANCLUB!

Look out for special offers on signed books, sports kit, merchandise (toys, stickers, pens – you name it!) and tickets to sporting events!

FLIP BACK THROUGH
THE LAST FEW
SECTIONS TO WATCH
THESE GUYS PLAY
RUGBY!